SOCCER STARS

SOCCER STARS

STORIES AND SKILLS FROM THE WORLD'S BEST PLAYERS

TRAVIS DiLEO

ILLUSTRATED BY
ANDERSON CARMAN

Z Kids • New York

Published in the United States by Z Kids, an imprint of Zeitgeist™
An imprint and division of Penguin Random House LLC
1745 Broadway, New York, NY 10019
penguinrandomhouse.com
zeitgeistpublishing.com

Zeitgeist™ is a trademark of Penguin Random House LLC.
ISBN: 9780593886151
Ebook ISBN: 9780593886069

Illustrations by Anderson Carman
Book design by Aimee Fleck
Author photograph © by Lori Brown
Edited by Angelica Martinez

Printed in the United States of America
The authorized representative in the EU for product safety and compliance
is Penguin Random House Ireland, Morrison Chambers, 32 Nassau Street,
Dublin D02 YH68, Ireland. https://eu-contact.penguin.ie
1st Printing

To my beautiful wife, Brittany, and our two children, Harper and Hallie, for believing in me

CONTENTS

INTRODUCTION
HEY, SOCCER FANS!

My name is Travis DiLeo. I am a soccer coach and lifelong fan of what is called "the beautiful game."

In today's big world, I've always felt soccer is the sport that can bring everyone together. No matter your age, background, or where you come from, we all speak the same language of football! Well, *soccer* in the US. I believe anyone, large or small, can become great at playing soccer.

I grew up admiring all the greats, like Zinedine Zidane, Diego Maradona, Thierry Henry, and Ronaldo Nazário. Like many of you, I dreamed of being like them when I was a kid. I admired their dedication, despite the obstacles they've faced, and how they've inspired the next generation of soccer players. You'll get to read about more greats in this book, and my hope is that their stories will show you that nothing can stand in the way of your dreams.

To become a truly great player, the ones we love to watch over and over, I believe there are two requirements: The first is the ability to overcome barriers. The second is the desire to make a lasting impression with a signature skill. To become well-known, a player must embody traits such as resilience, grit, persistence, self-belief, and an endless hunger to outwork the competition. All of these chosen players possess similar traits that led to great moments, legendary careers, and jaw-dropping skills.

In this book you will learn their signature skills and a little bit about *how* to use them in your next game. Reading about these soccer players is both motivating and fun. But most of all, I hope it inspires you to try out some of these skills on the field. Note that the signature skills described in this book are mostly designed to start on the right foot. If you favor your other foot, just switch left and right!

Focus on developing your technique from these soccer stars, and I promise you will thrive. Find the joy in playing, and everything else will come together.

Ready for kickoff? Let's begin!

PELÉ

BIRTH DATE
October 23, 1940

POSITION
Forward, Attacking Midfielder

HOMETOWN
Três Corações, Brazil

TEAMS
- Bauru (São Paulo)
- Santos FC
- New York Cosmos
- Brazil Men's National Team

TOP ACHIEVEMENTS
- Three-time World Cup Winner
- Youngest World Cup Winner
- 1999 Athlete of the Century
  (International Olympic Committee)

SIGNATURE SKILL
Bicycle Kick

ANY DISCUSSION ABOUT SOCCER USUALLY STARTS with the player considered to be the absolute best and the world's most recognizable—Pelé! Born Edson Arantes do Nascimento, he took his famous nickname from his favorite player, Bilé, which everyone mispronounced as Pelé.

Pelé was born into extreme poverty. His father taught him soccer by using a sock stuffed with newspaper as a ball. By the age of 13, Pelé played the fast-paced indoor version of soccer called *futsal*. He believed playing that style, especially against adults most of the time, allowed him to develop the ability to make quick and accurate decisions. He enjoyed competing with older players and testing out his skill against bigger, stronger people.

Pelé's soccer career began around the age of 15 with the Brazilian club Santos FC, where he quickly rose to the starting team. Shortly after, he was called up to the Brazilian national team. It was here that Pelé showed the world his soccer know-how. He could anticipate opponents, move around defenders with sudden changes of direction, and improvise on the field.

However, Pelé's natural talent was also a curse. He became the target of opposition players and was often roughed up during games. Always the team player, Pelé was happy to have lots of defenders focus on him while his teammates were left unmarked. In match after match, Pelé refused to allow his rivals the chance to take him out of his game. And despite his many accomplishments, Pelé did not believe in excessive celebration, as a sign of respect. He always met the opposition's anger with grace and sportsmanship.

Slowly, Pelé gained the admiration of his competition, ending much of the on-field trouble. Pelé simply loved the game and found joy on the field. He always played with a contagious smile on his face.

After he retired, Pelé became an ambassador of soccer and spent the rest of his life trying to unite people through what he called "the beautiful game." No matter where he went, Pelé was idolized. Fans would stand in long lines just to catch a glimpse of their hero. He strongly believed that soccer was far more than a sport and that it could unite the world, regardless of any barriers.

In 2018, he established the Pelé Foundation, a charitable organization that helps eliminate family poverty and increase youth education. Pelé's legacy is soccer greatness. However, if you could ask him how he wanted to be remembered, he would say something like, *I want people to know how much I care for children across the globe.*

BICYCLE KICK

You can't mention Pelé without thinking of the bicycle kick, originally created and credited to Brazilian great Leônidas da Silva. Pelé used the legendary strike to score in a 1976 Cosmos game against the Miami Toros. It is an acrobatic move, used when the ball is behind you and a normal shot is not possible. The best time to try it is from a pass into the penalty box. You must turn away from the goal and flip upside down to strike the ball. This skill can also be used to clear the ball away defensively, but it is primarily used to score breathtaking goals. This is a challenging maneuver and should be discussed with parents and coaches before you try it.

PHASE 1

Begin by leaning backward while lifting your left knee, circling both arms up and back, and positioning onto the toe of your right foot.

PHASE 2

Push off the ground with your right foot, lifting your body up.

PHASE 3

Next, continue rotating until the body turns parallel to the ground while beginning to switch leg positions using a bicycle motion.

PHASE 4

After completing one full bicycle movement, strike the ball using the laces of your right shoe.

PHASE 5

Finally, after striking the ball, you must immediately begin to prepare for a soft landing by rotating both of your arms downward and, if possible, turning to your left side.

JOHAN CRUYFF

BIRTH DATE
April 25, 1947

POSITION
Forward, Attacking Midfielder

HOMETOWN
Amsterdam, Netherlands

TEAMS
- Ajax Amsterdam
- FC Barcelona
- Washington Diplomats
- Netherlands Men's National Team

TOP ACHIEVEMENTS
- Nine-time Dutch Champion
- Six-time Dutch Cup Winner
- Three-time Euro Cup Winner

SIGNATURE SKILL
Cruyff Turn

HAVE YOU EVER HEARD THE SAYING "IF YOU GET knocked down, get back up"?

Johan Cruyff, a Dutch soccer legend, used this strategy time after time. He found ways to recover from the many setbacks thrown at him on his way to becoming one of soccer's greatest players and coaches. He is known as the father of modern football, widely viewed as the person most responsible for some of the greatest clubs in the world and for changing the way the game is played today.

Johan faced his first crisis at age 10 when he lost his father, who unexpectedly passed away from a heart attack. Johan did not let this tragedy derail him. Instead, he used it to honor his father's love of the game. Johan set the lofty goal of becoming a professional soccer player.

He knew he had plenty of work ahead of him, as he was small, thin, and not very fast. So how could he rise above all the talented players he would certainly face when competing for a spot on the local premier team? What could he do differently to stand apart from his rivals and impress the coaches?

Confronted with what he felt was a lack of natural abilities, Johan focused on *outworking* his competition. He trained in the basics, perfecting every skill as much as possible. He also studied the game so he could outthink his opponents and make better decisions on the field. It worked! By age 15, Johan became a standout player. Two years later, he made his debut for Ajax in his home country, the Netherlands. This was a key moment in Johan's life, launching a lengthy career of both national and international greatness.

Johan Cruyff's defining qualities are cemented in history: He understood that life is filled with difficulties on and off the field but believed in resilience most of all. He knew that how you face your problems can define how others view you. Finally, he recognized that a relentless work ethic was important to succeed and that outworking your competition can be more valuable than talent. In doing so, Johan Cruyff will always be remembered as a pioneer for revolutionizing the beautiful game of soccer.

CRUYFF TURN

If you are a player who likes to showcase your speed, this is the move for you. Its primary purpose is to change direction rapidly, leaving your defender going one way while you are headed the other. Johan first performed this skill in 1974 against Sweden. Shortly thereafter, it became known as the Cruyff Turn.

PHASE 1

Jump in front of and beyond the ball with your left foot.

PHASE 2

Land on your left foot and begin pivoting your body in the opposite direction, while your right leg is positioned on the outside of the ball.

PHASE 3

Using the inside of the big toe on your right foot, flick the ball toward your left side.

PHASE 4

To finish the move, shift your left foot out of the way and begin dribbling with your right foot.

MIA HAMM

BIRTH DATE
March 17, 1972

POSITION
Forward, Midfielder

HOMETOWN
Selma, Alabama, United States

TEAMS
- ⭐ University of North Carolina Tar Heels
- ⭐ Washington Freedom
- ⭐ United States Women's National Team

TOP ACHIEVEMENTS
- ⭐ Two-time Olympic Gold Medalist
- ⭐ Two-time World Cup Champion
- ⭐ Two-time FIFA Women's World Player of the Year

SIGNATURE SKILL
Upper 90 Power Shot

SOCIETY OFTEN SAYS LITTLE GIRLS ARE SUPPOSED TO be calm, quiet, and only interested in playing with dolls. They say girls can't play rough in sports, run fast, or compete against boys. Well, one little girl would prove that silly idea wrong. Meet Mia Hamm. Her impressive career changed the way the world forever looks at women's sports, especially women's soccer.

Mia's father was in the US Air Force, so her family moved around a lot. When they were stationed in Italy, a very young Mia saw her first soccer game. Even though she wasn't permitted to play organized soccer until she was five, Mia never hesitated to get out on the field anytime she could—and it was usually against boys. On one occasion Mia took the ball from a five-year-old boy, and she was barely two at the time! In junior high, she even played on the boys' American football team. Even as a kid, it was clear she had found a life-long passion for sports.

Mia's big break came when she was called up to the United States Women's National Team at age 15, one of the youngest ever. Just four years later she was invited to represent her country in the 1991 FIFA World Cup, where her play made a big difference. She scored the game-winning goal in a qualifying match against Sweden, setting the tone. Mia helped her team go undefeated in the tournament and capture the title of World Cup champions.

Moving around as a kid made it difficult for Mia to put down roots, make friends, and find a stable position on a good soccer team. But nothing came close to the difficulties she endured when her brother Garrett passed away from a rare illness. He was her inspiration to play sports, and he had persuaded her as a child to pursue her soccer ambitions. His passing occurred at the height of Mia's career, right in the middle of her World Cup and Olympic runs. This was devastating for Mia. But it also motivated her to make him proud, and she went on to win a second World Cup and Olympic Gold medal.

In addition to the strength Mia drew from her late brother, she possessed a burning desire to be the best female soccer player in the world. She was not interested in money or fame; she only wanted to be at the top of her sport. Mia believed you can accomplish anything with hard work and determination. Self-motivation and hours of training helped her achieve her goals. Mia believed that in order to succeed, you have to love the pain and the sacrifice it takes to get there.

Since her retirement, Mia has focused on inspiring young girls, showing them that anything is possible if you are willing to work for it. She understands that it's more difficult for women to climb the professional sports ladder and gain recognition. Mia has made it her mission to highlight female athletes across the world and build more opportunity with better pay. She led the way for American women and set the bar high, so if you want to reach the top, just do what Mia did—be tough and be determined!

UPPER 90 POWER SHOT

In soccer, coaches often say to aim for one of the four corners of the goal, which are all 90-degree angles. When shooting toward the upper portion of the goal, it's called the "upper 90 shot." The four corners are considered the most difficult areas for a goalie to stop the ball. These shots require great accuracy and power.

PHASE 1

The power for your shot comes from the sprint, or approach, to the ball. Ideally you should take three steps before shooting.

PHASE 2

This is your prep phase. At your last step, plant your left foot slightly in front of the ball while your kicking leg goes backward. Your kicking ankle is locked in position, preparing to strike the ball, while your left arm extends out for balance.

PHASE 3

This is the ball contact phase. Swing your leg to the ball, kicking either the center of the ball or slightly below center with your laces.

PHASE 4

This is the follow-through phase: Your kicking leg stays slightly bent the entire time, while your left arm crosses your body to increase power. Keep your head down. Fall forward toward the goal.

PHASE 5

This is the finishing phase. After striking the ball and following through, continue to push off of your left foot, eventually landing on your kicking foot. This push-off allows for your power to transfer through your shot.

LIONEL MESSI

BIRTH DATE
June 24, 1987

POSITION
Attacking Midfielder

HOMETOWN
Rosario, Argentina

TEAMS
- ⭐ Newell's Old Boys
- ⭐ FC Barcelona
- ⭐ Paris Saint-Germain
- ⭐ Inter Miami CF
- ⭐ Argentina Men's National Team

TOP ACHIEVEMENTS
- ⭐ 2022 World Cup Champion
- ⭐ Two-time Copa América Champion
- ⭐ Eight-time Ballon d'Or winner

SIGNATURE SKILL
Iniesta

STANDING AT A MERE FIVE FEET, SEVEN INCHES,
Lionel Messi is known as a giant on the soccer field. He is
one of the best dribblers and top goal scorers in soccer history. Lionel comes from a soccer-loving family who were all
involved with the game as players, coaches, and fans.

At four years old, he fell in love with the sport when
he played for a team coached by his father. Imagine
your father as both your parent and your coach—double
whammy! Fortunately, his grandmother was also a sup-
portive source of understanding and encouragement. To
this day he celebrates every goal by pointing up to the sky
to thank her for believing in him.

His next team was Newell's Old Boys club. The team
is also known as "the Machine of 87," named for the birth
year of its players. For three years the team was unbeat-
able. Messi made a big impression and began to find his
way as a standout goal scorer.

A few years later, at age 13, he was urged to move
to Spain by relatives who lived there so Lionel could
get a tryout for powerhouse FC Barcelona. At first, the
manager was very enthusiastic about Lionel, but he also
thought the boy was too young to sign. After Messi and
his family grew impatient and threatened to move back
to Argentina, Barcelona was afraid they would lose this
up-and-coming star, so they quickly made him an offer.
It happened so fast at a restaurant meeting that the
contract was written on a dinner napkin, just to make

sure their player would not get away! Lionel made his professional debut at age 17 and went on to establish himself as a dominant force for 17 years. It is safe to say FC Barcelona made a great decision!

Even though Lionel is one of the world's most famous soccer players, his life was not without challenges. Despite success in Europe, Leo (as he is often called) failed to accomplish his goals to win for his home country of Argentina.

Lionel was living in the shadow of his fellow countryman, the legendary player Diego Maradona, who led Argentina to the 1986 World Cup championship. Expectations for him grew with every failed international tournament. The pressure became almost impossible to handle. The constant comparisons were like playing against a ghost.

In the end, it was too much, and Lionel announced his international retirement in 2016. However, thanks to the encouragement of his coach, Lionel Scaloni, Messi returned to Argentina's national team after two months. Lionel played an important role in leading Argentina to two Copa América titles as well as the crown jewel of soccer, the World Cup, in 2022.

Lionel's restart was the result of his personal philosophies that he lives by on and off the field. He believes in surrounding himself with positive people and listening to their advice, like he did with his coach. But most important, Lionel is renowned for his specific goals and continuous learning, always mastering new skills. He is never satisfied with his performance, allowing him to constantly stay above his competition.

Messi's return after his brief international retirement shows how important it is to never give up or waver, even in the face of your challenges. His strong spirit highlights the need to believe in yourself, no matter what you choose to do in life!

INIESTA

Originally called "La Croqueta," this move was created by Michael Laudrup, but now it's known as the "Iniesta" after Andrés Iniesta. Lionel uses this skill in every game he plays. It makes professional defenders look like this is their first time on the field. It's designed to escape a defender when caught in a seemingly inescapable position. It's a reliable skill to perform when you're in a very tight spot while the ball is stationary or barely moving.

PHASE 1

Start with the ball positioned between your feet, which are approximately shoulder-width apart.

PHASE 2

Step to your left side, creating space from the ball, while your right foot slides closer to the outside of the ball.

PHASE 3

As the defender steps in to win the ball, rapidly shift the ball with a push (not a kick) from your right foot toward your left foot.

PHASE 4

Immediately after, your right foot will replace your left foot, while shifting your entire body to the side of the defender, creating a new lane to go past the defender.

PHASE 5

Then, simultaneously push off the ground with your right foot, and push (not kick) the ball with the inside of your left foot past the defender.

PHASE 6

Done at the right time and right speed, this move gives you more space for dribbling, a pass, or a shot.

TIM HOWARD

BIRTH DATE
March 6, 1979

POSITION
Goalkeeper

HOMETOWN
North Brunswick, New Jersey,
United States

TEAMS
- New York/New Jersey MetroStars
- Manchester United
- Everton FC
- Colorado Rapids
- Memphis 901
- United States Men's National Team

TOP ACHIEVEMENTS
- Two-time Gold Cup Winner
- FA Cup Winner
- Record 16 saves in 2014 FIFA World Cup

SIGNATURE SKILL
Kick Save

GOALIES MAY NOT ALWAYS BE THE STARS OF THE show, but that depends on where you're looking! After all, out of 11 players on the team, there is only one goalkeeper—and their performance can make or break the game. This is something Tim Howard, an American soccer star, learned when he was very young.

Tim was big for his age and tried a few sports, including soccer. To this day he admits he did not have any skills at first—he could not dribble or even pass the ball. The coach of his first team, the Rangers, sensed he might be good in another position, and wanted him to play goalie. But Tim didn't! He preferred to play up front, score, and be the hero.

During one game, Tim's coach asked him to play goalie for the first half, then play striker for the second half. This was quite a big challenge for Tim! He felt a great deal of pressure to stop shots and not let his team down. But he couldn't say no to his coach. He agreed, and by the end of the game he realized being a goalie was more fun and challenging. No surprise, his coach was right.

Around the age of 10, Tim's life began to change. He was diagnosed with Tourette syndrome, a condition that causes a person to do sudden tics, or movements. For example, you may feel a need to scratch your nose every time the phone dings. It can be very hard to deal with on a daily basis!

Tim's doctor gave him a bit of hope: He told Tim and his mom that every challenge has a flip side. Oftentimes, this condition causes people to become *super* focused. So Tim began to concentrate on soccer. He'd constantly watch professional soccer players on television, practicing their skills over and over again until he mastered them. Tim noticed his symptoms disappeared on the field. He was able to react much faster than the other players, providing the perfect advantage for a goalkeeper.

Tim eventually set a record of 16 saves against Belgium in the 2014 World Cup, but even more impressive was his 100-yard goal for Everton against Bolton during the 2011 Premier League season. He cleared the ball with a strong punt, which took a very unusual bounce over the heads of the opposition and into the net. Pretty impressive for a goalkeeper!

After retirement, Tim became a spokesman for children with Tourette syndrome, encouraging them to talk about their struggles. He established the Tim Howard Foundation, which provides resources for children with challenges, especially for those diagnosed with the same disorder. He led the way for Americans to break into European soccer and became the most decorated US Men's National Team goalkeeper. Tim's story shows that no matter what comes your way, there is always a path forward to win if you look for it!

KICK SAVE

The purpose of this reaction skill is to save a low shot directed at the goal, toward either the near or far post. The goalkeeper cuts the angle down and extends one foot to deflect the ball wide of the goal. Sometimes in practice coaches incorporate small-sided games, allowing field players to play goalie. So the next time you play against your sibling or best friend, you can be Tim Howard and send them home frustrated!

PHASE 1

Assume the striker is shooting to the far post. Close the angle on goal by sprinting in a crouched position toward the attacker with arms down and out, palms facing the attacker.

PHASE 2

Stay in a low position and begin turning your right knee down and inward.

PHASE 3

Your right knee is touching or almost touching the ground at this point.

PHASE 4

Extend your left leg out with your toe up, while keeping your hands in the same position.

PHASE 5

Rotate backward to allow for full leg extension and the best chance to get a touch on the ball as it travels toward the net.

ALEX MORGAN

BIRTH DATE
July 2, 1989

POSITION
Striker

HOMETOWN
San Dimas, California, United States

TEAMS
* Western New York Flash
* Tottenham Hotspur FC
* Orlando Pride
* San Diego Wave FC
* United States Women's National Team

TOP ACHIEVEMENTS
* Two-time World Cup Champion
* Two-time US Soccer's Female Athlete of the Year
* National Women's Soccer League's 2022 Golden Boot winner

SIGNATURE SKILL
Volley

THE US WOMEN'S NATIONAL TEAM STANDOUT ALEX

Morgan began playing soccer with her local American Youth Soccer Organization (AYSO) team in Diamond Bar, California. The experience made such an impact on her that when she was seven years old, Alex gave her mom a Post-it declaring she was going to be a professional soccer player. After a few years of having fun with her friends on the pitch, Alex joined a program for developing youth soccer players. She said the experience helped her gain skills and much-needed game minutes.

In college at the University of California, Berkeley, Alex became an elite goal scorer. She led her team in goals all four years. She played professionally on a number of big-name club teams, but her real claim to fame came from her time on the US Women's National Team, appearing in four World Cups and three Olympic games.

Alex was only 20 years old when she was called up to the women's national team. The pressure of sharing the field with many of her heroes was almost too much to handle. Even though she was living her dream (and what she'd written on that Post-it years before!), she found herself overwhelmed with stress and anxiety at the thought of playing with some of the best female athletes in the nation.

Adjusting to new surroundings and coaches can be scary for young athletes, and Alex was no exception. Alex knew she'd have to work through her fears to succeed. She started listening to her inner voice. She kept telling herself that she *could* compete at this level, the opposite of what her fears were telling her. She focused on rebuilding her confidence, which she knew had gotten her this far.

Her dedication paid off: Alex proved to be a reliable teammate and worthy of representing her country on the world stage. Alex's time on the US national team resulted in two World Cup championships as well as two Olympic medals: one gold and one bronze.

Sometimes life presents you with special moments that can change your future. Alex had such a moment as a teenager when she met national team player Joy Fawcett after a game. Alex asked for a photo, but it took 10 tries to capture the picture because the camera was not working. "Those two minutes impacted me so much," Alex said, according to the *Los Angeles Times*. She was overwhelmed by Fawcett's patience, and from that moment on, Alex understood the importance of giving back to the fans and to those who support her.

As an adult, she established the Alex Morgan Foundation with the primary mission of creating equality for women in athletics and in life. The foundation works on solutions for needy communities through sports, especially through soccer. Since retirement, Alex has been devoted to showing young players that belief in yourself, no matter how much doubt and fear you face, can carry you all the way to your dreams and beyond.

SIGNATURE SKILL
VOLLEY

A volley is when you strike a soccer ball while it is bouncing. This skill is difficult because it requires technique and timing. There are many types of volleys, but we will focus on one. When done correctly, these shots are some of the most beautiful goals in soccer.

PHASE 1

During this prep phase (part one), you must judge the bounce and speed of the ball. Juggle or kick the ball around a bit and notice how slowly or quickly the ball comes back to you.

PHASE 2

During prep phase (part two), turn your body in the direction of the ball headed toward you.

PHASE 3

Put your support arm up and out for balance, and bring your kicking leg back with your ankle locked, while also leaning toward your right side.

PHASE 4

Swing your left leg and strike the ball slightly above center to prevent the ball from going too high. Your chest should also come toward the ball during this phase.

PHASE 5

Follow through with control, while bringing your right arm across your body for more power.

PHASE 6

After striking the ball, land on your kicking foot to maximize power.

CHRISTIAN PULISIC

BIRTH DATE
September 18, 1998

POSITION
Winger, Attacking Midfielder

HOMETOWN
Hershey, Pennsylvania, United States

TEAMS
- Borussia Dortmund
- Chelsea FC
- AC Milan
- United States Men's National Team

TOP ACHIEVEMENTS
- Champions League winner
- UEFA Super Cup winner
- Captain of the US Men's National Team

SIGNATURE SKILL
Cut Inside and Back Post Curl

CHRISTIAN PULISIC HAS ESTABLISHED HIMSELF AS
one of the best soccer players in the United States, the English Premier League, and Serie A league. His career began at age seven when his family moved to England because of his mother's work. Christian lived there for only a year, but it was enough time to ignite his desire and start him on his way. (Funnily enough, his mom and dad met while playing soccer in college.)

At 13 years old, Christian began playing for the US Under-15 Men's Youth National Team, where he progressed quickly. His quick skills triggered a careful look by the European clubs. In fact, one German club, Borussia Dortmund, made him an offer to play overseas. Christian joined the team but also found it tough to move so far from home—he was still a kid at the time. Even though it was hard being away from friends and family, this decision launched his career.

After tearing it up on the pitch with a string of stellar performances for Dortmund, Christian made his way back to America when he was called up to the US Men's National Team. He became known as a goal-scoring machine and caught the attention of the English Premier League club Chelsea. At the time, the team signed him to one of their highest-paid contracts.

Christian's rapid rise was not without obstacles. His calm but fearless style of play has often put him in dangerous positions. Defenders usually took the opportunity to rough him up. Unfortunately, this resulted in a parade of injuries throughout his career, creating constant challenges both physically and psychologically. Living away in unfamiliar surroundings made it even harder.

Whenever Christian got injured, he would take time to heal so he could get back on the field. But he experienced a number of other issues in addition to his physical pain. He found it difficult to avoid the fear that naturally comes with any type of injury: *Will I be the same? Can it happen again? How do I protect myself?* All of these questions rolled through his mind. His managers and teammates often wondered the same things. Christian felt overwhelmed and frustrated.

Captain America, as Christian is known on the US Men's National Team, needed to find a way to break the cycle of being sidelined. He also needed to lessen the anxiety he felt because of his injuries. That's when he decided to talk to a therapist about his worries.

Christian has said that single decision helped him tremendously and that talking to someone isn't anything shameful. Talking out your problems improves feelings and begins the healing process, particularly when you share your issues with someone you trust, like a coach or teammate. Christian has been clear that his team and those around him played a big part in healing his physical injuries as well as removing his fear of getting hurt again.

Currently, Christian plays for an Italian club, AC Milan,

but he also works to inspire children and youth players closer to home. He has partnered with PUMA to form the Christian Pulisic Legacy Program, an organization dedicated to serving underprivileged children in North America who want to play soccer. Christian's story is one of courage and the will to overcome life's hurdles.

CUT INSIDE AND BACK POST CURL

This is a difficult skill, but if you are a determined player who wants to make the highlight reel, then this is a *must* to learn. It is designed to create space and bend the ball away from the goalkeeper toward the far post. Other than a bicycle kick, this is one of the prettiest goals you can score in soccer matches. During a match against Bolivia, Christian scored a terrific goal in the third minute, giving the USA the start they were looking for.

PHASE 1

Begin by dribbling sideways toward the goal, while simultaneously looking up at the goalie to check for the best spot to shoot.

PHASE 2

Next, take one to two fast steps toward the ball and bring the kicking leg back, while maintaining the parallel position to the goal.

PHASE 3

Strike the outside of the ball with the inside of your big toe, which begins the spinning motion of the ball.

PHASE 4

Strike the ball with full force and follow through with a straight leg.

PHASE 5

Quickly bend your kicking leg to allow for the rotation of the ball.

PHASE 6

Your momentum should carry you to your right side and backward, away from the goal, exposing your chest toward the open net, allowing for the ball to bend toward the upper right side of the goal.

SALMA PARALLUELO

BIRTH DATE
November 13, 2003

POSITION
Forward

HOMETOWN
Zaragoza, Spain

TEAMS
- ★ UD San José Zaragoza
- ★ Zaragoza CFF
- ★ Villarreal CF
- ★ FC Barcelona
- ★ Spain Women's National Team

TOP ACHIEVEMENTS
- ★ 2018 FIFA U-17 Women's World Cup Champion
- ★ 2022 FIFA U-20 World Cup Champion
- ★ 2023 FIFA World Cup Champion

SIGNATURE SKILL
Single Feint and Far Post Strike

BEING TALENTED IN MULTIPLE SPORTS IS A GOOD
thing, right? It's definitely something to be proud of.
However, to make it in the big leagues, there may come a
time when you have to choose one sport to focus on. That
can be a stressful experience. That is exactly what happened to Salma Paralluelo, a rising soccer star.

Salma has two brothers who are both very good athletes. They encouraged their sister to participate in sports.
Early on, Salma recognized her exceptional speed: Almost
every time she raced her siblings, she won!

Salma's happy childhood was interrupted when her
father lost his job. As the family struggled financially,
Salma found comfort in sports, first in track and then in
soccer. The more she played, the more she dedicated herself to training and competing. As a perfectionist, Salma
would put the same effort into schoolwork and training,
often requiring waking up at five a.m. just to keep up with
her assignments.

As a teenager, Salma was captain of her soccer team
while also achieving massive success on the track. She
became a national track champion, setting several records.
Salma felt like she could pursue two sports and do equally
well at both. In 2019, she signed with her first professional
soccer club, Villarreal, partly because the team allowed her
to continue competing in track.

Then, in 2021, a string of bad injuries, including a
severe knee tear, hampered her performance. Salma was

faced with the difficult decision of choosing between soccer and track. This was not easy for Salma, to give up something she really liked to do and commit to one sport.

During her injury rehabilitation, she accepted a contract with Barcelona. Salma understood that in order to do something great, she had to focus on a single purpose—and believe in herself. Salma made a good choice. She became a standout player for Barcelona and helped Spain's women's national team win three FIFA World Cups in three different age divisions. Salma was the first player to ever do so!

During rehab for her injuries, Salma learned that her choices shape her reality. The worst decision she could make was to do nothing and risk failing at both soccer and track. Instead, she trusted her judgment. Now she is one of the best young players in women's professional soccer.

SINGLE FEINT AND FAR POST STRIKE

At the highest level in soccer, the simple moves tend to work best. The easiest move in soccer is the single feint. Basically, you step one way and then run the other. It has a very high success rate in games, as you can do this skill at slow or high speeds. Also, you can use it to go past defenders or create space for a shot on goal like Salma!

PHASE 1

The single feint starts with a fast step to your right, slightly in front of the ball.

PHASE 2

As you bring your left foot inside to change direction, the defender has just processed your initial step with your right foot (which is a delayed reaction).

PHASE 3

Meanwhile, you begin an immediate shift to your left, pushing the ball off at a slight angle away from goal using the outside of your foot.

PHASE 4

Step beyond the ball with your right foot. Bring your right arm out for balance, and position your left leg back in preparation to shoot to the far low post.

PHASE 5

You will now strike the ball slightly above center with the inside of your big toe, while turning your foot slightly outward to allow for this.

PHASE 6

Follow through strongly with your kicking leg toward the far low corner.

VINÍCIUS JÚNIOR

BIRTH DATE
July 12, 2000

POSITION
Winger

HOMETOWN
São Gonçalo, Brazil

TEAMS
- ★ CR Flamengo
- ★ Real Madrid
- ★ Brazil Men's National Team

TOP ACHIEVEMENTS
- ★ Two-time Champions League winner
- ★ Three-time La Liga winner
- ★ 2023–24 UEFA Champions League Player of the Season

SIGNATURE SKILL
Inside Cut

IMAGINE GROWING UP IN BRAZIL, DREAMING OF
becoming a great soccer player. Then, after years of hard work, you become one of the best players in the world, only to be called mean names on the field solely because of the color of your skin. Meet Vinícius Júnior—or Vini Jr., as he is often called.

Vini Jr. was born in São Gonçalo, Brazil. When he was six, his dad introduced him to futsal, the indoor form of soccer (yes, the same sport Pelé played!). It was not long before the future star found he was good at the indoor game, but he loved the outdoor version much more. By age seven, Vini Jr. was part of a youth multisport program called Flamengo. From there, he began to showcase his exceptional skills.

Vini Jr.'s quickness and ability to dribble with pace was so remarkable, defenders simply could not keep up with him. Within five years he debuted with Flamengo's top soccer team. It was here that Vini Jr. made a big impression on one of the most famous soccer clubs in the world, Real Madrid. He signed with the Spanish powerhouse, and by his early twenties, Vini Jr. was named a Real Madrid starter.

Arriving as a star player for one of the best clubs on the planet was a dream come true for Vini Jr. But once he got on the field, he started to battle more than the opposition's defenders. In a game against Valencia, bullies in the stands began to shout inappropriate words at him related to his skin color. This sparked an eruption of insults, and several more people in the stands began chanting terrible names at him. They also made harassing gestures directed right at Vini Jr., reducing him to tears. Stadium announcers warned the spectators to settle down, but not much else was done. This caused Vini Jr. to lose his cool with another player. He got a red card and was forced to leave the game. At that moment, he vowed to make it his mission to fight discrimination and prejudice within the soccer community.

The incident might've pushed him to the world stage, but it was Vini Jr.'s skill that made him rated as the number one player in the world by many. Even though soccer is his passion, Vini Jr. believes he can and should also be a force for equality, paving the way for those that follow.

"I have a purpose in life," Vini Jr. said on Twitter, "and if I have to keep suffering so that future generations will not have to go through these types of situations, I'm ready and prepared."

In 2021, Vini Jr. established the Vini Jr. Institute, which provides educational opportunities for underprivileged Brazilian communities. When FIFA formed a special anti-racism player committee, they chose Vini Jr. to lead it. Brazil also approved a new "Vini Jr. law" to combat racism at sporting events—stopping or suspending matches for bad conduct.

Though he discovered his talent on the soccer field, Vini Jr. quickly embraced the higher calling to defeat discrimination. This player believes winning does indeed matter, but it is more important to stand up for your beliefs. His story is a true example of how you can achieve success while being a voice for the greater good.

SIGNATURE SKILL
INSIDE CUT

When you go fishing, you put bait on the hook to bring the fish closer. That's the same idea with this move. The beginning part of this move is the bait, drawing the defender in close with a move called a roll. Then, as the defender is ready to bite, you cut inside and sprint past. This move is most effective when you are in wide areas near the touchline. The defender is more likely to take the bait in those positions.

PHASE 1

This is the bait, part one. Turn toward the defender and gently put your right foot on the ball.

PHASE 2

This is the bait, part two. Roll your right foot forward, which allows it to come down on the ground with the ball moving forward slowly.

PHASE 3

Next, take a big step with your left foot. Start turning your body toward the touchline in preparation for your inside cut.

PHASE 4

As the defender goes for the ball, step with your right leg. Your right foot goes beyond the ball and turns inward toward the touchline. Your hips rotate toward the touchline as well.

PHASE 5

The defender swings and misses, and you are clear to go down the touchline.

PHASE 6

As the defender's foot comes down trying to reclaim their balance, you are already sprinting in a fast dribble toward goal.

CRISTIANO RONALDO

BIRTH DATE
February 5, 1985

POSITION
Winger, Forward

HOMETOWN
Funchal, Madeira, Portugal

TEAMS
- ★ Manchester United
- ★ Real Madrid
- ★ Juventus FC
- ★ Al Nassr FC
- ★ Portugal Men's National Team

TOP ACHIEVEMENTS
- ★ 2016 Euro winner
- ★ Five-time Ballon d'Or winner
- ★ Five-time Champions League winner

SIGNATURE SKILL
Ronaldo Chop

CRISTIANO RONALDO IS WIDELY RECOGNIZED AS
one of the best soccer players—ever! At age three, he was introduced to the sport and quickly loved everything about it. When you look at all his successes, it's hard to believe his early life was filled with challenges.

When he was a child, Cristiano was raised in extreme poverty. He often had to ask for food at local restaurants just to get by. On top of this, he was diagnosed with a heart condition. This would be enough to crush most young boys' dreams, but not Cristiano. As a teenager, he underwent successful surgery to treat his heart problem. The average person needs weeks to heal—Cristiano stunned his doctors and resumed training just a few days after the surgery!

He saw his difficulties as motivation to ignite a desire to do better. Cristiano dedicated himself night and day to practice, train, and perfect his soccer skills so he could eventually have a better life for himself and his family.

When he was 12, Cristiano made the tough decision to leave his family on the island of Madeira and head to the Portuguese mainland to join the Sporting CP Youth Academy. Living alone and trying to showcase his skills was hard as he struggled to keep up with his studies. As he became a better player, Cristiano could earn a good living playing professional soccer. He made the tough choice to leave school because he knew playing the game full-time would let him finally support his family.

At the age of 17, Cristiano earned a starting position on Sporting CP's adult team and then caught the eye of Manchester United's Sir Alex Ferguson. The legendary manager wasted no time signing the young player, recognizing how special he would become. Cristiano went on to be a star forward with Manchester United and later with Real Madrid. After winning the top club tournament five times, he became known as "Mr. Champions League." Among all of his achievements, Cristiano considers playing for the Portugal men's national team his greatest honor.

Cristiano's climb to the professional ranks and international stardom was achieved thanks to his unbreakable spirit in the face of health difficulties. Cristiano's philosophy is simple—choose your goal, believe in yourself, and have the discipline to work hard for it. Cristiano works to build physical stamina *and* to build his mental strength. He knows that in order to win, you have to train even when you don't feel like it. Examples include going for a run when you want to play video games or choosing to drink water instead of drinking soda. If you want to chase your dreams, follow Cristiano's inspiring example of dedicated effort and unending commitment!

RONALDO CHOP

Ronaldo first became famous using this move when he played for Manchester United. Visually it's a lot like the Cruyff Turn, with the same outcome to rapidly change direction. The main difference is that you are not slowing down. Your goal is to maintain your speed and rapidly change direction toward the center of the field closer to the goal. To feel like Ronaldo when you play, after you score, yell "SIUUUU!!!"

PHASE 1

As you dribble at full speed, step with your left foot beside the ball while your right leg bends.

PHASE 2

Then instantly jump off your left foot, while simultaneously letting your right leg drift to the right in the air.

PHASE 3

Your left foot lands beyond the ball, allowing room for the inside of your right foot to kick (chop) the ball sideways to your left.

PHASE 4

At this point, your legs are temporarily crossed. In order to maintain full speed, your feet must land simultaneously.

PHASE 5

Finish the move by stepping with your left leg toward the ball into a full-speed dribble. You must keep your knees bent and hips low to the ground in order to rotate and sprint in the new direction of the ball.

CONCLUSION
GOOOOOAL!

Imagine it's minute 88 in a big match. You are in the box, hoping to score. Suddenly, a volley comes in from your winger, but you are out of position with your back to the keeper. You think of Pelé, and boom, you strike the ball with a bicycle kick. Goooooal!!

There is a reason soccer is the most popular international sport and the most watched across the world. Time and again fans go absolutely bonkers during the World Cup to see their favorite team compete. "The beautiful game," as Pelé called it, is a terrific physical activity that anyone can do. However, the biggest reason to play is that soccer is just plain fun!

You have now been introduced to 10 players who achieved their dreams through hard work, learning from their mistakes, and, most important, belief in themselves. Without exception, each of them had faith in their abilities and refused to give up on their dreams. From Cristiano's Ronaldo Chop to Lionel's Iniesta to Mia's upper 90 power shot, these signature skills can be learned and used on the pitch. All it requires is determination and practice—a lot of it.

My best advice to you is to be consistent and work on your skills every chance you get. You can train during team practices, or simply grab a ball, find some space, and give it a go. As you keep at it, your game will improve, and your confidence will soar! Finally, do not miss a chance to watch the big matches with the top players, because seeing is believing. The more you become a fan, the more you will be inspired to unleash the great player inside of you!

Check out the extras at the end of this book to keep having fun with these players, on and off the field.

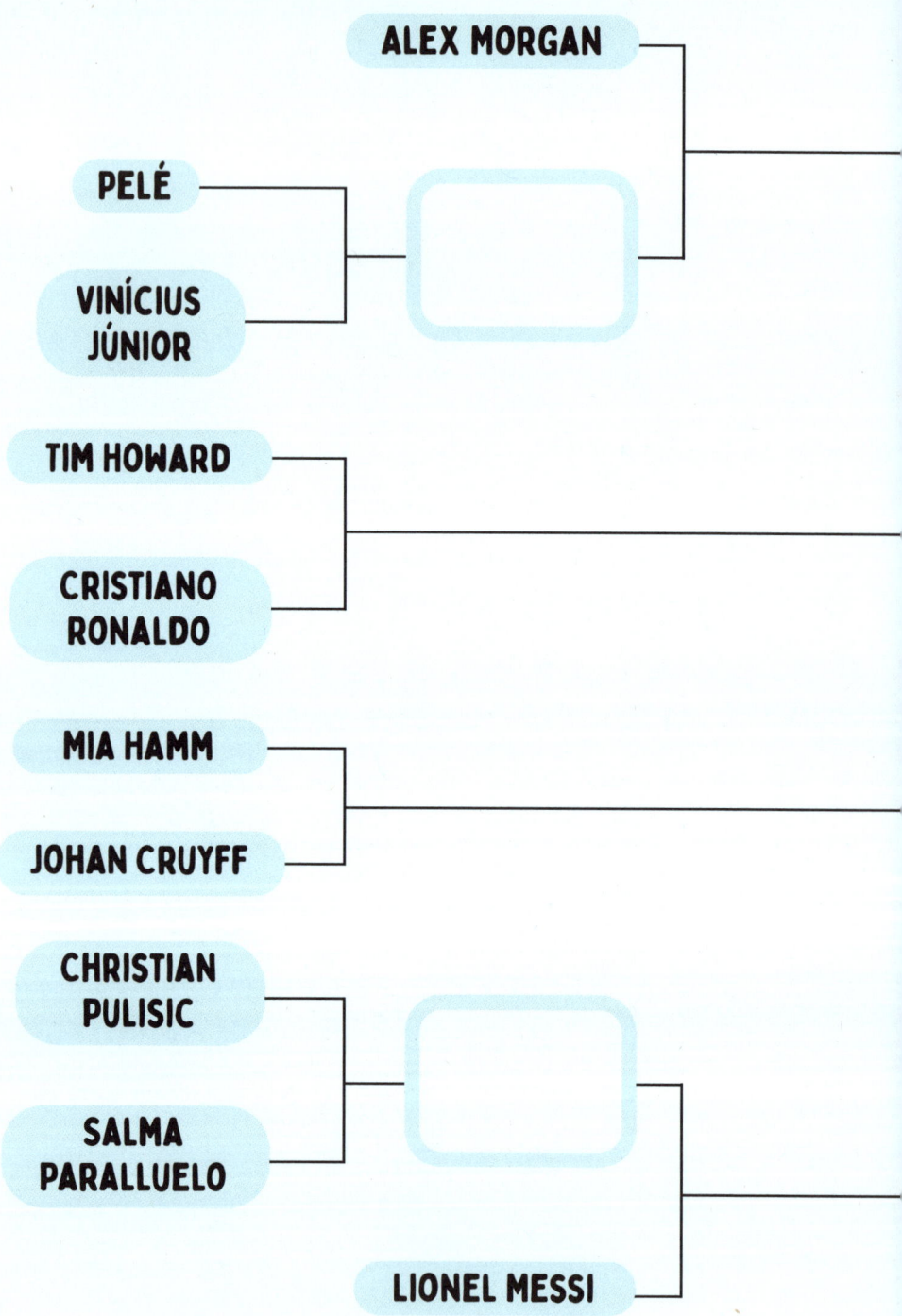

ALEX MORGAN

PELÉ

VINÍCIUS JÚNIOR

TIM HOWARD

CRISTIANO RONALDO

MIA HAMM

JOHAN CRUYFF

CHRISTIAN PULISIC

SALMA PARALLUELO

LIONEL MESSI

WHO'S YOUR FAVORITE PLAYER?

MY FAVORITE PLAYER IS...

MOVES I'VE TRIED

☐ Bicycle Kick

☐ Cruyff Turn

☐ Upper 90 Power Shot

☐ Iniesta

☐ Kick Save

☐ Volley

☐ Cut Inside and Back Post Curl

☐ Single Feint and Far Post Strike

☐ Inside Cut

☐ Ronaldo Chop

ACKNOWLEDGMENTS

I am deeply grateful to my father, Stephen, for guiding me with his lifelong expertise in writing.

I am blessed to have the patience and love of my wife, Brittany, and two beautiful daughters, Harper and Hallie, who have sacrificed so much so that I may pursue my ambitions. You are my world.

To my mother, Lucy, and sister, Kristin, I am thankful for your unending encouragement to overcome and to be the best. I want to recognize my coaches, teammates, friends, and soccer families for their unwavering support.

I would also like to express my sincere appreciation to Zeitgeist for giving me the opportunity of a lifetime to write this book.

ABOUT THE AUTHOR

TRAVIS DiLEO is an exercise physiologist with a bachelor's degree in kinesiology from Penn State University and a master's degree in exercise science from the University of Pittsburgh. He is a certified strength and conditioning specialist (CSCS) and USA weightlifting instructor (USAW). Travis has played soccer at the club, classic, high school, and collegiate level. He has coached soccer at Penn State Altoona and for the Pittsburgh Riverhounds

Academy. He is a former Centers for Disease Control (CDC) scientist who coauthored an award-winning project that helped Ebola health care workers stay safe.

In 2019, Travis launched his youth development school, TD Soccer Performance Academy. The mission of the academy is to maximize the potential of serious players through a unique and scientific approach. In 2023, he launched his online VIP Soccer Analysis Program, where through technology and science he can analyze, diagnose problems, and transform players from anywhere in the world.

Travis is passionate about soccer and most important, he is devoted to raising the level of competition for youth programs in the United States. He resides in central Pennsylvania with his wife and two young daughters.

Parents, you can follow Travis on Instagram @soccercoachtrav and learn more about his VIP courses and online training at soccercoachtrav.com.

ABOUT THE ILLUSTRATOR

ANDERSON CARMAN graduated from Savannah College of Art and Design with a BFA in sequential art. He is the creator and artist of *Fear Hunters*, *Cyber League Baseball*, and *Stan, the Green Flamingo*. He lives in Atlanta, Georgia, with his wife and three kids. One time he juggled a soccer ball over 300 times. Too bad no one was around to see it.

Hi, parents and caregivers,

We hope your child enjoyed *Soccer Stars*. If you have any questions or concerns about this book, or have received a damaged copy, please contact customerservice@penguinrandomhouse.com. We're here and happy to help.

Also, please consider writing a review on your favorite retailer's website to let others know what you and your child thought of the book!

Sincerely,
The Zeitgeist Team

01 14